Store Window Design

Store Window Design

LOFT

Editorial coordinator: Cristina Paredes

Texts: Sandra Moya

Art director: Mireia Casanovas Soley

Layout: Jonathan Roura, Nacho Gracia Blanco

Translation: Jay Noden

Editorial project:

2007 © LOFT Publications
Via Laietana, 32, 4° Of. 92
08003 Barcelona, Spain
Tel.: +34 932 688 088
Fax: +34 932 687 073
loft@loftpublications.com
www.loftpublications.com

ISBN 978-84-95832-72-6
Printed in China

Index

Introduction

Introduction

Welcome to the 21st century, marked by consumerism, as the 19th and 20th were before it. The Industrial Revolution, the passage of time, the introduction of new technologies, the appearance, development and "boom" of new work positions, the inclusion of women in the work force... All this has contributed to an increase in both the demand and supply of work, and consequently a rise in family income levels. Consumption levels have also subsequently risen, to the extent that today we do not only buy for necessity, we also do so for pleasure.

Consumption has increased and so, therefore, has the number of stores and the amount of products on the market. Rivals are born encouraging competition between brands and establishments. How are businesses to survive in such a highly competitive market? They must attract attention, encourage possible customers to approach their product; the product they are offering. The problem, logically, is how to gain consumer confidence when today's frenetic pace of life does not afford us the time to wander around all the stores within our reach.

This is why the store window, which until relatively recently was not considered particularly significant, has gained so much importance in recent years, Today, however, it is a key element, as it has the power to gain clientele.

Store window design has become an art. New fashions, originality of designs, the possibility of combining a multitude of materials... And, as the famous French painter, George Braque, says "progress in art is not a question of pushing limits, but getting to know them better". We must discover and master all elements that may be of use to us when designing a store window as this will allow us to create spaces, which, despite being reduced in size, have their own character, and represent what is on offer inside. When we decide to go shopping we do so in our free time, time

Camper London | Martí Guixé | 1998 | Photography © Inga Knölke
Maison Hermès Tokyo | Renzo Piano/Rena Dumas Architecture Intérieure | 2001 | Photography © Michel Denancé

for us to discover the different store windows on display. This is when store window design comes into its own. The stores have to sell their products, which enter our minds through our eyes, in a game of seduction. This is indeed a perfect definition. The products are decorated and the accessories, the colors used throughout our stage and the combination of lights, are all there to attract our attention. The whole scene entices you into thinking that what you are seeing is indeed what you are looking for, it is just what you needed, and at last you've found it. The store window has fulfilled its role and accomplished its objective with perfection: it caught your attention and lured you in. The store window, without you realizing, has whisked you away to another world. A world you have been wanting to go to, where you can be assured of finding all you were looking for. You have been drawn to the products in that window and not the one next door or across the street. It is vitally important to understand that a customer's choice to enter one shop over another depends, almost entirely, on what is on offer in the window. And this is why store window design has become such a key element in the 21st century.

Mango Basel | Damián Sánchez | 2001 | Photography © Joan Mundó
Prada Epicenter New York | Rem Koolhaas/OMA | 2001 | Photography © OMA

Prada Epicenter New York | Rem Koolhaas/OMA | 2001 | Photography © OMA

The History

Store window design did not begin to take on importance until after the Industrial Revolution, when people's needs and incomes changed. Its true relevance was apparent from the 19th century onwards, as before this time there were no enclosed spaces dedicated to commerce. All shopping was done in market places, which, in some villages and cities, took place on a weekly basis in the streets or the town square. In those days, the low standard of living meant people focused on having the basic necessities for survival, and would not even have dreamt of luxuries and satisfying pleasures. Consumerism did not exist, as people were unable to spend more than what was strictly necessary to reach the end of the month.

But with the development of industry, the work situation changed. Until then labor was mostly focused on the land, on agriculture. The arrival of factories increased the amount of personnel in the cities. Peasants logically emigrated in order to improve their conditions, in search of a brighter future. Work conditions improved, salaries went up, along with the average family income, allowing people to consider acquiring more than just what was basic to survive. Secondary necessities could be fulfilled, i.e. buying for pleasure. Thus consumerism was born.

People could buy more, and so it became necessary to maximize the production of goods, and minimize the time it took. Businesses had to offer a quality product, which was also cheap, or at least cheaper than other available products, as by this time there was already talk of competition. The industrialization had changed people's way of life, their priorities and the social structures. The feudal lords became the Bourgeoisie, i.e. factory owners who were powerful and rich; while the peasants became workers with improved, more dignified qualities of life, thanks to the increase in their incomes.

Gianni Versace New York | Gluckman Mayner Architects | 2000 | Photography © Lidia Gould
Y's Yohji Yamamoto Boutique Copenhague | Svendborg+Balsborg | 2001 | Photography © Station l/Adam Mørk

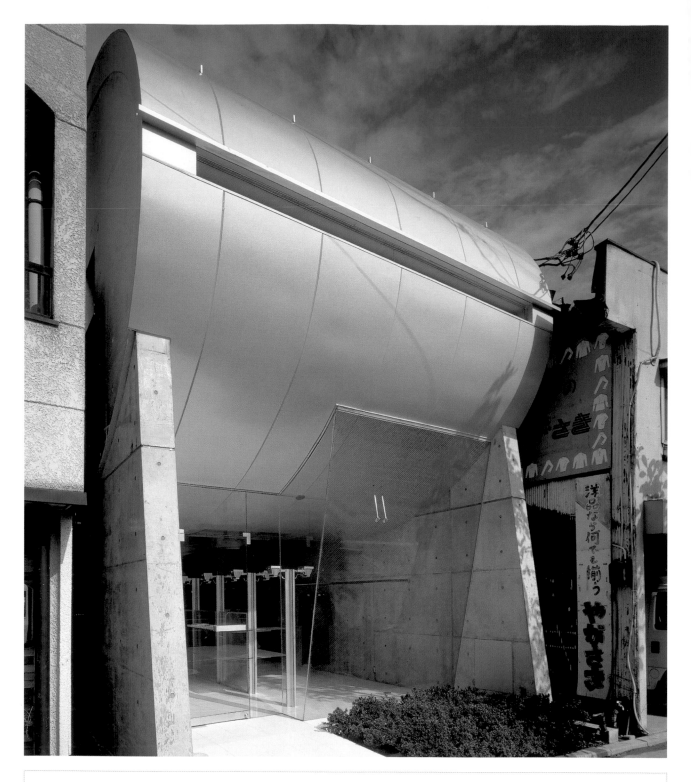

La Ciénega | Hideo Yasui | 1998 | Photography © Nacása & Partners

Tehen New York | Daniel Goldner Architects | 2000 | Photography © Michael Moran

Camper London | Martí Guixé | 1998 | Photography © Inja Knölke
Yves Saint Laurent Paris | Gluckman Mayner Architects | 2001 | Photography © Lidia Gould

Gianni Versace New York | Gluckman Mayner Architects | 2000 | Photography © Lidia Gould

The Bourgeoisie created a capitalist, industrial world, where commerce played an increasingly important role. Workers earned more but spent double, so the need arose to create and offer as many products as was possible, products that people were unaware even existed until that time, but which, thanks to new technologies, were now within everyone's reach. This manufacturing together with a growth in exports of merchandise from far away and exotic lands increased the need for enclosed spaces dedicated exclusively to commerce.

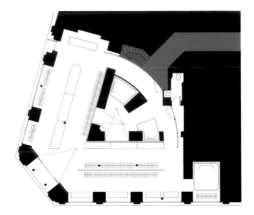

Yves Saint Laurent Paris | Gluckman Mayner Architects | 2001 | Photography © Lidia Gould

Gianni Versace New York | Gluckman Mayner Architects | 2000 | Photography © Lidia Gould

Y's Yohji Yamamoto Boutique Copenhague | Svendborg+Balsborg | 2001 | Photography © Station I/Adam Mørk

Store Windows vs Architecture

Shopping, during the industrialization, was no longer just out of necessity. Priorities had changed, and from then on fulfilling dreams and buying products that would satisfy personal pleasures, also acquired an important role.

As we have already said, the need arose to create spaces dedicated solely to commerce, spaces which would offer all products in existence. Shopping had become a leisure activity, a pastime, and stores began to set up in the same area, thereby attracting buyers to that place. Once there, the challenge was on for businesses to seek customers' approval, what they offered and how they offered it could either attract consumers or put them off. This need to gain clientele appeared a long time ago, but logically it is still the case today only with even more intensity, as there is now a much greater supply of products.

The Industrial Revolution and the massive influx of people coming from the country lead to the need for creating homes to accommodate everyone. In the cities it was not possible to house a family in a single building, and areas had to be set up that could house as many inhabitants as possible. Blocks of flats solved this problem, and businesses would set themselves up on the ground floors. New structures were put in place and visiting shops, which previously could not even have been imagined, became an everyday occurrence. People had direct access to the stores, whose windows offered endless products, until then unknown to the workers, and which were now within their grasps.

There was no time to wander around and go shopping; the day was dedicated exclusively to work. This was, and still is, why the store window was so important. It has to be situated in a key position of the building, where it will be noticed and will instantly attract attention; it has to make immediately clear what is sold inside, and last but by no means least, it has to have elements that set it apart from the rest in order for us to choose this place, and not the store across the street.

Nicole Farhi Flagship New York | Gabellani Associates | 1999 | Photography © Paul Warchol
Jil Sander Paris | Gabellani Associates | 1995 | Photography © Paul Warchol

Modelo Taylor's Shop Barcelona | GCA Arquitectes Associats | 1997 | Photography © Jordi Miralles
Ferragamo Venedig | Gabellani Associates | 2000 | Photography © Paul Warchol

Jil Sander Paris | Gabellani Associates | 1995 | Photography © Paul Warchol

So we cannot speak of store windows without also speaking of architecture. They are two elements which are mutually exclusive. One cannot be understood without the other. The importance consumerism has today has made shop owners opt for large, open buildings and spaces, which allow for designs that are unique and different to anything else. Spaces that allow us to combine shapes, and which provide us with enough room for us to create our stage.

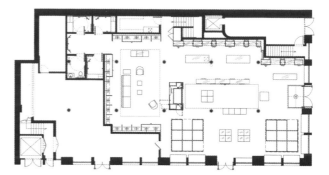

Chanel Boutique New York | Peter Marino | 2000 | Photography © David Cardelús

Modelo Taylor's Shop Barcelona | GCA Arquitectes Associats | 1997 | Photography © Jordi Miralles

Maison Hermès Tokyo | Renzo Piano/Rena Dumas Architecture Intérieure | 2001 | Photography © Michel Denancé

Maison Hermès Tokyo | Renzo Piano/Rena Dumas Architecture Intérieure | 2001 | Photography © Michel Denancé

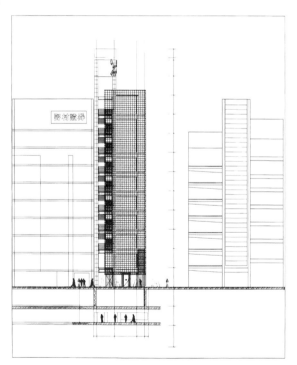

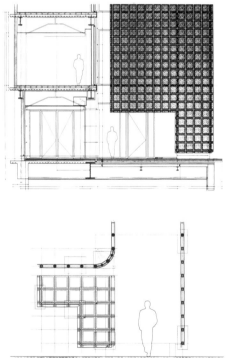

Maison Hermès Tokyo | Renzo Piano/Rena Dumas Architecture Intérieure | 2001 | Photography © Michel Denancé

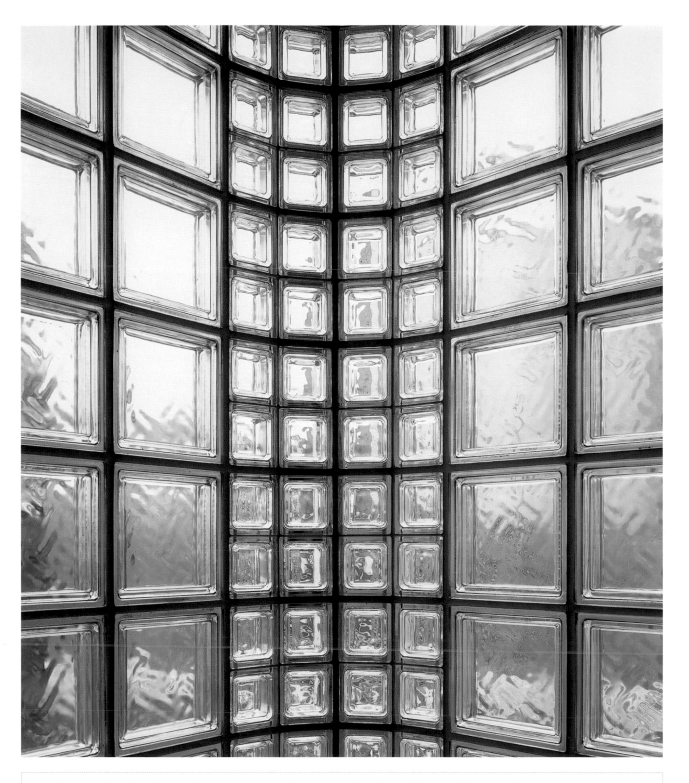

Maison Hermès Tokyo | Renzo Piano/Rena Dumas Architecture Intérieure | 2001 | Photography © Michel Denancé

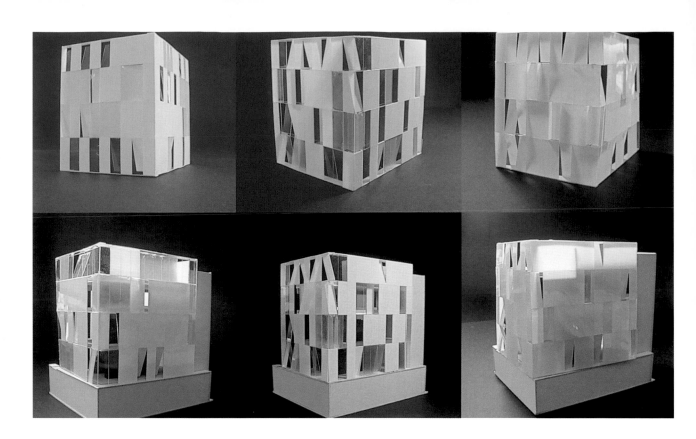

Helmut Lang Tokyo | Gluckman Mayner Architects | 2002 | Photography © Jock/Esto

Helmut Lang Tokyo | Gluckman Mayner Architects | 2002 | Photography © Jock/Esto

Drawing Attention

The establishment of stores led, in the mid 19th century, to the appearance of fixed prices for products, and the idea of bartering for and exchanging goods disappeared. Shops had become big business, and their owners were only interested in the profits needed to fulfill their secondary needs, their dreams. Today this premise is even more apparent, due to the large amount of stores, and has given rise to what is known as the game of seduction.

The store window must attract customers and its role is paramount since it must display the product and persuade the potential buyer. The space has to be alive and to communicate it must be attractive and provocative. Nobody will enter a store whose product display does not offer something different.

The decoration and design of a store window, therefore, is not as simple as it looks. Everything is relevant, from the lighting to the choice of colors, the fabrics used to current fashions. We could say that creativity is a store window's most important characteristic, our starting point. The space must be original, different from the rest. Something, which until then has not been done, and will therefore guarantee the attention of possible customers. As well as this, the aforementioned elements also play a vital role. We need to understand the different lighting techniques; the psychology of color; in other words which tone is most appropriate for a given situation; to be up-to-date with current fashions and bear in mind which season we are in; the design of a store window will change depending on whether it is winter, autumn, spring or summer.

Fashions, consumers and products are constantly changing, and the store windows have to adapt to this evolution in order not to fall behind and lose customers who may be attracted by the many other store

Jil Sander San Francisco | Gabellini Associates | 1996 | Photography © Paul Warchol

Mango Mataró | Damián Sánchez | 2000 | Photography © Taku

windows on offer. What does a store window need to attract people's attention? There has to be a striking visual impact, something that at a glance, in just a second, is unforgettable. The products must, therefore, be part of an attractive display. Ideas must be clear in order to create a simple space, which reveals what is on offer inside. We should avoid anything that overloads the space, distracting the customer from the actual product. The aim is to ensnare customers and increase sales, and the creativity and imagination reflected in the store window will determine sales results in an increasingly competitive market.

Jil Sander San Francisco | Gabellini Associates | 1996 | Photography © Paul Warchol

Ultimo San Francisco | Gabellini Associates | 1997 | Photography © Paul Warchol

Mango Barcelona | Damián Sánchez | 2000 | Photography © TAKU
Prada Epicenter New York | Rem Koolhaas/OMA | 2001 | Photography © OMA

Prada Epicenter New York | Rem Koolhaas/OMA | 2001 | Photography © OMA

Gokaldas Images New York | I-Beam Design | 2000 | Photography © Killian Mattitsch

Helmut Lang Boutique New York | Gluckman Mayner Architects | 1997 | Photography © Paul Warchol

Sephora Barcelona | Patrick Genard, Gerard Gasmi & Chafik Gasmi | 2000 | Photography © Eugeni Pons

Chanel Paris | Peter Marino & Associates | Photography © David Cardelús

The Product

The Industrial Revolution helped to change our concept of the product, which until then was not given nearly as much importance as it is today. In the Middle Ages money didn't exist, and nor did the amount of products that we are now so used to. All that was important was to survive, and even commerce was not then, as we know it now. Product exchange was the dominant form of commerce: animals for vegetables, eggs for an item of clothing... but then came industrialization and with it the development of technologies, the inclusion of new products, which were no longer limited to fulfilling basic needs, and the appearance of money, putting an end to the exchange of goods.

The ways of doing business have indeed changed. Stores have appeared and the market places in the villages have slowly disappeared, but what has never changed is the product in itself. Although many more have appeared, its importance has been the same throughout the ages. Market places, fairs, stores and shopping malls have been created with a single purpose in mind: to offer products. These are the stars of the consumerist world we live in. The sole aim is to sell the product, and be more favorably accepted than the competition.

The only difference between the products sold today and those on offer in the Middle Ages is the "quality". In those days you could find handcrafted products sold by the craftsmen themselves. No two products were the same as they were made one by one, and this gave them a special touch. Nowadays this touch is practically non-existent as all products are mass-produced, hundreds are made at a time because quality is no longer the most important thing. Today is all about selling and satisfying demand.

Superga Shops | Massimo Iosa Ghini | 1997 | Photography © Santi Caleca

Superga Shops | Massimo Iosa Ghini | 1997 | Photography © Santi Caleca

Yanko Boutique Barcelona | GCA Arquitectes Associats | 1997 | Photography © Jordi Miralles
Desso Showroom Waalwij | Van Esveld Dierdorp Design Associates | 2001 | Photography © Frank Tielemans

The Martin's Valaoritou Athens | Zege | 2001 | Photography © V. Makris

Tardini Store New York | Fabio Novembre | 2001 | Photography © Alberto Ferrero

The Establishment

Once it is clear that the product is the key element, it's time to work. It must reach the customer by way of our game of seduction.

The first place to display our products is the store window, which, given the amount of competition today, often takes up the entire façade of the establishment. Since the 19th century the inclusion of glass, steel, new technologies such as lighting and the psychology of colors has been vital here, as they have allowed store windows to gain much more importance and relevance in terms of showing the product. Their function is to sell the product in a matter of seconds, a form of advertising that must be exploited to the full.

We must take full advantage of the possibilities that glass offers. Most stores, except those found in shopping malls, are located in the street, so we can take full advantage of the natural light. This means we should avoid dark or excessively garish colors as they distract the customers' attention and take importance from the product, which we must never forget should always be the star of the show. The store window should use straight lines, which connect the reality in the street with the fantasy and magic we want people to find inside our establishment.

Reference has been made to steel and new technologies. Steel and aluminum have given new decorative touches not only to the windows, but also to buildings' structures, providing a modern flavor that had previously not existed. The advent of electricity has offered the possibility to play with the lighting, which is fundamental in shopping malls where there is practically no natural light at all. In these cases the light can raise (or not) the importance of our product, by using different intensities and colors to attract peoples' attention. For stores located in the streets, as

Y's Yohji Yamamoto Boutique Copenhague | Svendborg+Balsborg **|** 2001 **|** Photography © Station I/Adam Mørk

Donna by The Martin's Valaoritou Athens | Zege | 2000 | Photography © V. Makris

Nicole Farhi Flagship | Gabellini Associates | 1999 | Photography © Paul Warchol
Ultimo San Francisco | Gabellini Associates | 1997 | Photography © Paul Warchol

The Martin's Valaoritou Athens | Zege | 2001 | Photography © V. Makris

Amaya Arzuaga Madrid | Francesc Pons | 2000 | Photography | © Raimón Solà

Gil Vienna | Propeller Z | 2000 | Photography © Margherita Spiluttini

has already been mentioned, natural light plays a fundamental role and artificial lighting can help to give a special touch or to show what is on offer in a different way, when daylight no longer plays a part.

But what we must remember nowadays is that the store window is not limited to merely the area at the entrance to the store. The interior has now also been converted into a massive display window, which needs to be as attractive or more so than that found at the entrance. The architect, in this case, acquires a significant role in creating a space for the owners that will seduce customers from the moment they enter.

Once the design has been built, we must focus on the layout of the spaces. Functionality is important – we must never forget that the product is the star – but neither must we forget about our game of seduction that must be present throughout the space. Fashions and product designs change, and establishments must adapt if they do not want to fall behind and lose customers. When considering the establishment it is important to bear in mind that both the store window and the interior must adapt to changing times, designs and fashions. An increasingly informed and demanding public needs to be offered an attractive store.

Mandarina Duck Barcelona | Fubert S.L. | 2001 | Photography © Eugeni Pons

Dior Beverly Hills | Peter Marino | 2001 | Photography © Paul Warchol

Tardini Store New York | Fabio Novembre | 2001 | Photography © Alberto Ferrero

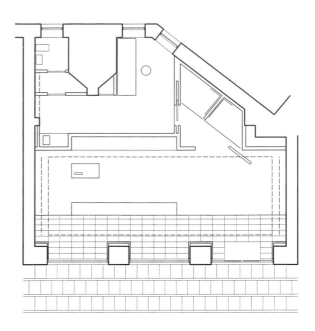

Y's Yohji Yamamoto Boutique Copenhague | Svendborg+Balsborg | 2001 | Photography © Station I/Adam Mørk

Y's Yohji Yamamoto Boutique Copenhague | Svendborg+Balsborg | 2001 | Photography © Station I/Adam Mørk

Giorgio Armani Milan | Claudio Silvestrin Architects | Photography © Matteo Piazza
Ferragamo Venecia | Gabellini Associates | 2000 | Photography © Paul Warchol

Helmut Lang Parfumerie New York | Gluckman Mayner Architects | 2001 | Photography © Lidia Gould

the Architects and the contrac... ...ently working on a uniq... ...o the best job possib... ...roject to refurbish this spa... ...erefore it will take a minimum of six months to complete. Bei... small company, we cannot afford to be closed for such a lo... ...eriod of time. We also feel that a closed store in such an interesti... ...nvironment is not fair to our colleagues. So, in the meantine, ...re opening this WALK IN PROGRESS STORE. We hope that you w... ...nderstand that although shoeboxes are not lavish, the conce... ...s simple, useful and recyclable. The shoes are ...he new CAMPER store will open in September 200...

Temporary States

Adapting to Seasons

The product is what matters most. That is clear. But the design and decoration of the store window and an establishment's interior has a life span and is subject to constant changes and renovations, adapting to the different seasons and new fashions that appear on a regular basis. When a store window is created we know that before long it will disappear, its life is limited to, at most, a few months. It does not have the luxury of surviving much more than that because otherwise we run the risk of losing customers.

The reality is that commerce today is ephemeral and the store windows therefore have to be easily adapted to this premise. For this reason a growing number of store owners are contracting specialists in store window design, who have the job of constantly studying market tendencies, to be able to quickly design appropriate display windows. Adapt or die. This is the only way a product can survive in an increasingly competitive world.

To adapt to the times the place where the display window is situated must be sufficiently flexible, as we will not always be using the same elements. On some occasions more furnishings or more lighting will be needed and we have to be prepared for this, and, furthermore, know how to adapt to the different seasons. The Christmas window will not be the same as on Saint Valentines or Mother's day, businesses must adapt to all the different festivities. The same is the case for the different seasons. When summer is about to start the store window will not be the same as when it is winter. Once again, the objective is to sell the product throughout the year, and to do this the window must undergo constant renovation.

Yves Saint Laurent New York | Gluckman Mayner Architects | 2001 | Photography © Lidia Gould
Camisería Pons Barcelona | Enric Sagnier | 2001 | Photography © Nuria Fuentes

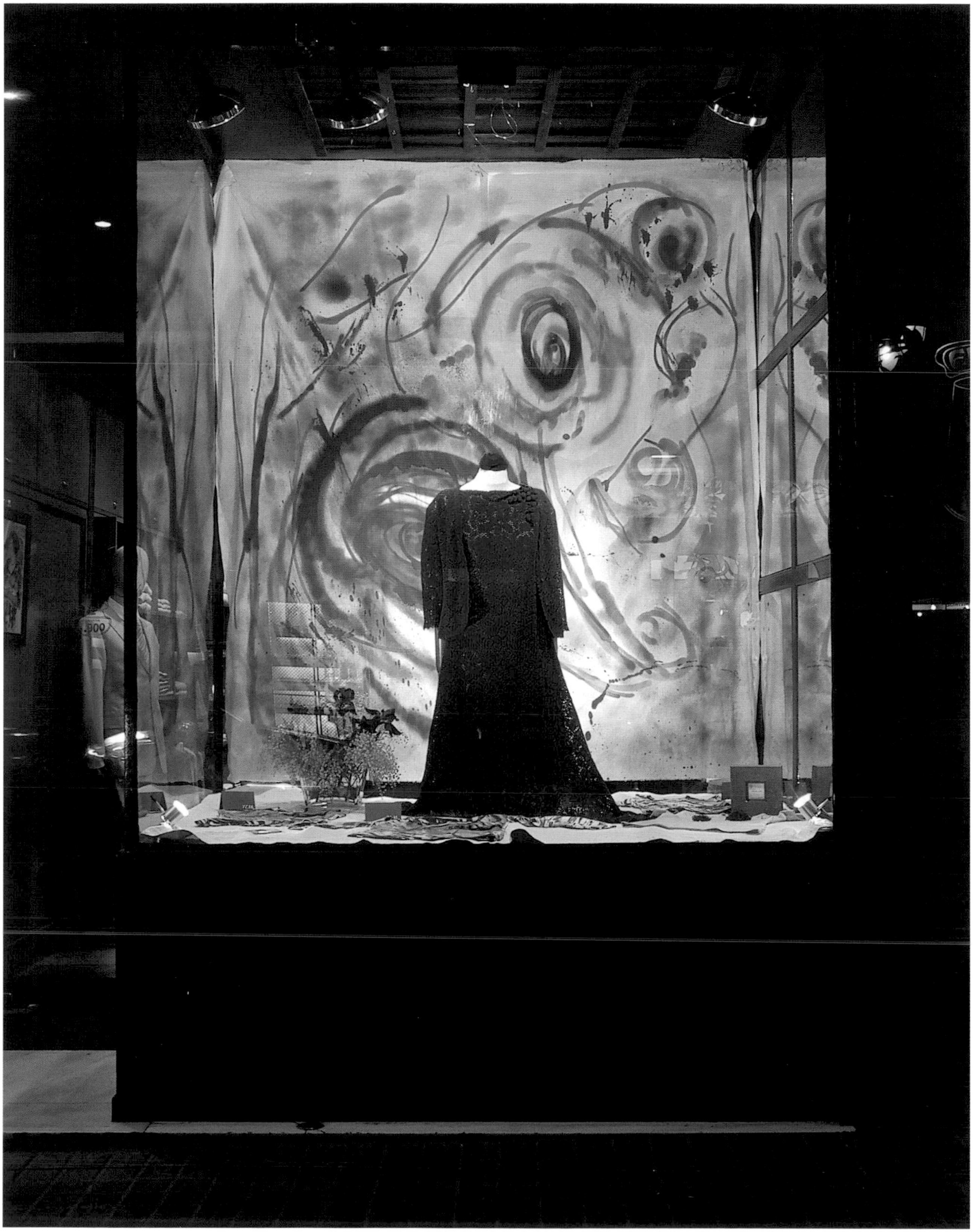

Prada Epicenter New York | Rem Koolhaas/OMA | 2001 | Photography © OMA

Yves Saint Laurent New York | Gluckman Mayner Architects | 2001 | Photography © Lidia Gould
Factor Dental Barcelona | Manuel Ortiz | 1999 | Photography © Jordi Miralles

Helmut Lang Boutique New York | Gluckman Mayner Architects | 1997 | Photography © Paul Warchol

The Importance of Design

The store window transmits a message; it must communicate quickly and clearly with the customer, but not only this. It also has to give some detail or characteristics of what can be found within the establishment.

As we have already pointed out, the potential customer is increasingly well informed and demands much more, since today's needs have changed radically. We have already spoken about how we are now surrounded by a multitude of products, many of which are practically identical, and for this reason we have to decide between them. Our choice, in many cases, will depend on the design of the different establishments, who, regardless of the time of year, must come up with a design that will maximize the potential clientele. This is why it is very important that the different establishments are clear about what type of public they are looking for, as they do not all have the same objectives. Some stores want to attract young people, others aim

for a clientele with higher purchasing power, some simply aim for as many of the public as possible. The design of a store's interior, the furnishings used and the aesthetics of the decorations must all quickly indicate what type of establishment we are entering.

We must bear in mind that, contrary to popular belief, our references to store windows and design do not just mean clothes stores. Nowadays design is relevant for pharmacies, bookshops, franchises, perfume shops... All types of shop, today, must aim to please, in order for their products to survive among the competition. Although the interior of the store is fundamental, as we have just explained, the real responsibility of attracting clientele to enter an establishment still lies with the store window. Regardless of the time of year, this is the first place where the products are displayed and this is where the game of seduction begins.

Camper New York | Martí Guixé | 2000 | Photography © Inga Knölke

Camper New York | Martí Guixé | 2000 | Photography © Inga Knölke

Fendi Roma | Lazzarini & Pickering | Photography © Matteo Piazza

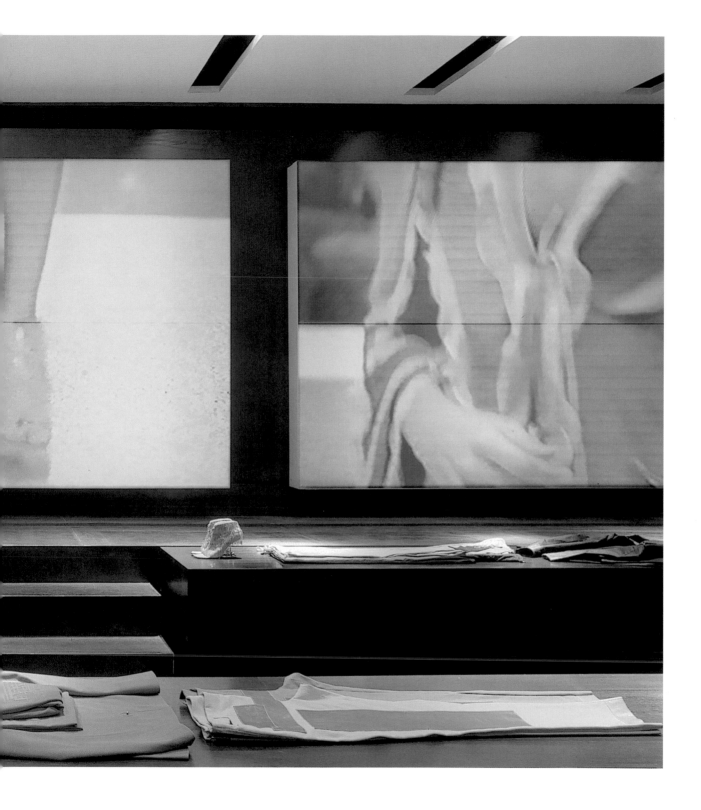

Toyota Showroom Girona | Montserrat Nogués | 2001 | Photography © Eugeni Pons

Prada Epicenter New York | Rem Koolhaas/OMA | 2001 | Photography © OMA

Ferragamo New York | Gabellini Associates | 2000 | Photography © Paul Warchol
Nicole Farhi Flagship New York | Gabellini Associates | 1999 | Photography © Paul Warchol
Mango Basilea | Damián Sánchez | 2001 | Photography © Joan Mundó

Prada Epicenter New York | Rem Koolhaas/OMA | 2001 | Photography © OMA

Marketing as a Weapon of Seduction

Given the vast amount of similar products on the market today, brands need to be able to tip the balance when consumers come to choosing between their product or that of a competitor. But it is not so easy to create a brand, as not all are accepted in such a highly competitive market. Some brands take years before appearing on the market. It is fundamental, first of all, to research the market thoroughly, consider the possible customers, the competition and the influence their presence may have. The brand may then enter the market and hopefully gain a public loyal enough to stay with them for generations.

The brand, in the end, is what makes our product special, and what marks the difference with respect to the rest of the competition. To accomplish this objective we have the marketing department. This is responsible for creating a line to follow, in other words, they give a product a particular image and personality. Their aim is for this image and personality to attract attention and interest among possible customers, and for these customers to remember this image and immediately connect it with the product.

The importance a brand can attain is such that it may mean a rise in the product's value, that its price increases within the category it has been placed in. Today we are under the impression that the more expensive the product, the higher its quality.

But we cannot speak of brands without making at least a brief reference to the so-called "own brand", that which belongs to a chain of retailers, i.e. a supermarket. This brand can sell a multitude of products under the name of the supermarket, with the sole aim of gaining loyal clientele. The advantage of this system is that the products that carry the supermarket brand are often more economical, and the distribution and advertising costs are lower.

The development of the brand made it necessary to look for small symbols or pictures that would represent the product, in order not to have to always use the name. This was how the logo was created, which became the

Dior Beverly Hills | Peter Marino | 2001 | Photography © Paul Warchol
Chanel Boutique Osaka | Peter Marino | 2001 | Photography © Paul Warchol

representation of the brand and visual identity of the company. Its aim is to transmit a message of well-being, reliability and good quality, with respect to the product it represents. But the correct use of a logo has to go hand-in-hand with the strategic plan of the marketing department, as the marketing campaign and its dominant colors carry a great deal of importance. For example, a small yellow shield with a horse drawn on it, says nothing to us, yet if we connect it with the color red, we immediately relate it to Ferrari.

We must also bear in mind that when we speak about a logo, we are speaking of an icon and a name. The

Cacao Sampaka Barcelona | Antoni Arola | 2001 | Photography © Eugeni Pons
Superga Shops | Massimo Iosa Ghini | 1997 | Photography © Santi Caleca

Ferrari Store Maranello | Massimo Iosa Ghini | 2001 | Photography © Santi Caleca

Ferrari Store Maranello | Massimo Iosa Ghini | 2001 | Photography © Santi Caleca

Helmut Lang Parfumerie New York | Gluckman Mayner Architects | 2001 | Photography © Lidia Gould
Cafe Donna The Martin's Valaoritou Athens | Zege | 2000 | Photography © V. Makris

Mango Basilea | Damián Sánchez | 2001 | Photography © Joan Mundó

icon becomes the visual symbol for the brand and the name is its phonetic representation. This can be seen more clearly through an example. Nike is the brand name, the name of the company, and its symbol, which is known by everyone, is its icon. What is important is for the brand to identify the product and attempt to gain loyal customers.

This marketing plan, which has been followed throughout the creation and design of a brand and its corresponding logo, must continue in the establishment where the product is to be sold. The most important thing is for the customer to quickly associate a logo or a color with a particular product in order to gain their loyalty. It is all part of a well-researched strategic plan. This is where the so-called corporative image comes into play, something that goes beyond aesthetics and attempts to create an emotional bond between customers and the product in order to increase clientele. The corporate identity is important because it leads the customer through a market, flooded by products similar to their own, and because it gives the brand personality.

This marketing plan – the creation of the brand, the birth of the logo and the corporate identity – finishes with the establishment in which we are going to sell the product. Today all companies look for spaces that open onto the street, in other words, that occupy a building's ground floor, as this is where the opportuni-

Y's Yohji Yamamoto Boutique Copenhague | Svendborg+Balsborg | 2001 | Photography © Station I/Adam Mørk

Y's Yohji Yamamoto Boutique Copenhague | Svendborg+Balsborg | 2001 | Photography © Station I/Adam Mørk

ties lie for elaborating window displays to attract customers' attention. There are even brands and companies with so much power and importance among their clientele that they create a base establishment, i.e. a store that acts as a reference to others that form part of the same company but are smaller. This can be seen, for example, with large clothes stores. The world's most important designers have their headquarters in Paris or New York, the stores that offer everything they create. However they are still present in the rest of the world, installing small stores in Barcelona, Milan or London, where they offer products from the current season.

We must be aware that the image of a store is what helps to sway us towards a particular product. This is why the design and decorative style of the interior is so important. We have already mentioned that the first thing to attract the customer is the window, as it is the first thing they will see. However the attention and expectations this achieves must be upheld inside the establishment. The needs of the 21st century have changed, we no longer just buy for necessity, we also do so for pleasure and fun, so establishments, both small stores and large shopping malls, adapt to these times and look for spectacular designs. Any tiny detail, that may appear of little relevance, becomes fundamental in achieving our objective: to sell the product.

Chanel Boutique Frankfurt | Peter Marino | 2000 | Photography © Nikolas Koenig

Chanel Boutique Osaka | Peter Marino & Associates Architects | 2001 | Photography © Paul Warchol

Yanko Boutique Barcelona | GCA Arquitectes Associats | 1997 | Photography © Jordi Miralles

Dior Beverly Hills | Peter Marino | 2001 | Photography © Paul Warchol

The Point of Sales

Shopping and More

The place where we set up an establishment is no longer merely a place we use to distribute our product. Since the end of the 19th century, with the development of new technologies and a new form of commercial exchange, the point of sales has taken on growing importance. It also has to help us sell the product, act as support; its image needs to attract potential customers. To do this extensive research needs to be carried out into what we have. In other words, we need to know what space is available to us to be able to then come up with a design that adapts to personal tastes and forms a perfect complement with the image of the brand, without forgetting that the prime objective is to attract attention from the very first second.

Today's market is so competitive that the smallest detail is important for survival. A good product needs to be created, which does not carry an excessively high price in order to be within everyone's reach. And to do this it is important that the company communicates with the customers, which is done through the point of sales. And so the establishment is acquiring more and more importance. It is becoming increasingly common to find stores where, as well as finding particular products, there are different activities going on which attract the customer's attention: presentations of new products, exhibitions, displays… Today it is quite common to enter a library and find a corner where you can have a coffee while reading the newspaper. They are new marketing strategies with the sole aim of gaining loyal customers, and they usually succeed.

But how do you make customers realize on first sight that inside this establishment there are more options

Factor Dental Barcelona | Manuel Ortiz | 1999 | Photography © Jordi Miralles
Desso Showroom Waalwij | Van Esveld Dierdorp Design Associates | 2001 | Photography © Frank Tielemans

that just buying the product? This is the job of the store window. This is no longer just a place to display the product, it must have a life of its own, offering a glimpse of what lies inside without being excessively explicit. It must follow the decorative line of the rest of the store, as it is extremely important to give an image of continuity, of coherence, to avoid confusing customers. We need to try to integrate the window with its surroundings, making it another space within the establishment, something that attracts people's attention and is not limited to just displaying the product that is on offer inside.

Tardini Store New York | Fabio Novembre | 2001 | Photography © Alberto Ferrero
Prada Epicenter New York | Rem Koolhaas/OMA | 2001 | Photography © OMA

Superga Shops | Massimo Iosa Ghini | 1997 | Photography © Santi Caleca

Camper New York | Martí Guixé | 2000 | Photography © Inga Knölke

MEDITERRANEAN STYLE:
We live in a specific environment. We are influenced by the culture, history and landscape that surround us. Camper was born in Mallorca, a small island in the Mediterranean, one of the richest and most culturally diverse areas on Planet Earth.

CAMPER MEANS PEASA
in Catalan, a language sp
million people in Europe.
recreating a rustic old pe
the insides and outsides
This word (camper) defin
Our dream is to walk very

How to Seduce

The need for the store window to integrate with the design followed throughout the store means we have to be constantly attentive to changes in fashions. The premise of the store window is "renovate or die", we have to survive in a world plagued by competition and gain customers every second. Many things have evolved and adapted to lifestyles, and establishments, as we have already seen, are at the top of the list.

This also extends to store windows. From its style, distribution, decoration and even its use of small details, we know what the company is like that has created the product in front of us. It must be given personality to make it unique and different from the rest. The store window must continually adapt in any way necessary. Functionality is another of its most important characteristics. On many occasions the space available to us for installing a window display is minimal and it must become a dynamic, flexible space, that allows, when needed, for the introduction of extra furnishings; and for the use of different materials… The idea is to find practical solutions for the space we have, without forgetting the current design and new fashions that must be reflected if we want to attract attention.

But you cannot seduce with just the design and distribution of the different elements of a space. We need to consider how to position these elements; the decorative style is another important weapon of seduction and helps to define what type of product is being offered and to what type of public. A store could opt for a classical style, linked, for example, with antique stores; a romantic style for all products related with the home; a more contemporary decoration for clothes stores for young people or stores that offer leisure products; or a more minimalist style where the product takes precedence, such as in a furniture store. We will now look at decorative styles and their influences.

Ultimo San Francisco | Gabellini Associates | 1997 | Photography © Paul Warchol

Jil Sander Paris | Gabellini Associates | 1995 | Photography © Paul Warchol

Maison Hermès Tokyo | Renzo Piano/Rena Dumas Architecture Intérieure | 2001 | Photography © Michel Denancé

Yves Saint Laurent Paris | Gluckman Mayner Architects | 2001 | Photography © Jacques Cravard
Sephora Barcelona | Patrick Genard, Gerard Gasmi and Chafik Gasmi | 2000 | Photography © Jordi Miralles

Carolina Herrera Madrid | GCA Arquitectes Associats | 2000 | Photography © Jordi Miralles

Helmut Lang Boutique New York | Gluckman Mayner Architects | 1997 | Photography © Paul Warchol

The Martin's Valaoritou Athens | Zege | 2001 | Photography © V. Makris
Jil Sander Paris | Gabellini Associates | 1995 | Photography © Paul Warchol

Donna by The Martin's Valaoritou Athens | Zege | 2000 | Photography © V. Makris

René Lezard New York | 1100 Architects | 1997 | Photography © Michael Moran

Weathervane Santa Mónica | Sant Architects | Photography © John Edward Linden

Decorative Styles

We must never forget that the most important thing is to attract the customer. Working from this premise we need to bear in mind that the decorative line inside of the point of sales needs to be reflected in the window, if we are going to follow our strategic plan. We must follow a coherent line to generate confidence in our product.

To achieve this objective it is fundamental to give the store window style. A style that the brand, and in other words the product, possesses. This is how we achieve a window with its own life. It must be perfectly clear that one style is not necessarily better than another, when it comes to the window display. They are all good options, there are no rules to follow, as even combining classical elements with more innovative ones can be acceptable.

We can opt for a classical/romantic style, for elements that never seem to go out of fashion. A style known for its sobriety, elegance and sophistication often dominated by the use of wood, i.e. for window frames, the mannequins and for the choice of furnishings. This decorative style is both beautiful and harmonious, and transmits a sense of tranquility. For this purpose light colors are often used that increase the luminosity and sensation of fragility. It is a style found in clothes stores for people with greater purchasing power, in certain furniture shops, jewelers…

If we prefer a more modern and up-to-date decor,

Big Net Vienna | René Chavanne | 2001 | Photography © Hélène Bignet

120

The Martin's Valaoritou Athens | Zege | 2001 | Photography © V. Makris

then a more contemporary and minimalist style may be suitable. The premise of this style is "less is more", it avoids all unnecessary elements that merely distract the customer's attention, and for this reason it is a style found in abundance in today's store windows. It is dominated by simple lines that delineate and take full advantage of the space, and can be decorated with any colors, as long as the contrast is not excessively shocking, as this may tire the eyes and deter customers. Where can this decorative style be found? In fashion stores for young people and children, gift or bookstores, cell phone retailers...

Louis Vuitton Beverly Hills | Peter Marino | 1999 | Photography © David Cardelús
Mandarina Duck Barcelona | Fubert | 2001 | Photography © Eugeni Pons

Camper New York | Martí Guixé | 2000 | Photography © Inga Knölke

Prada Epicenter New York | Rem Koolhaas/OMA | 2001 | Photography © OMA

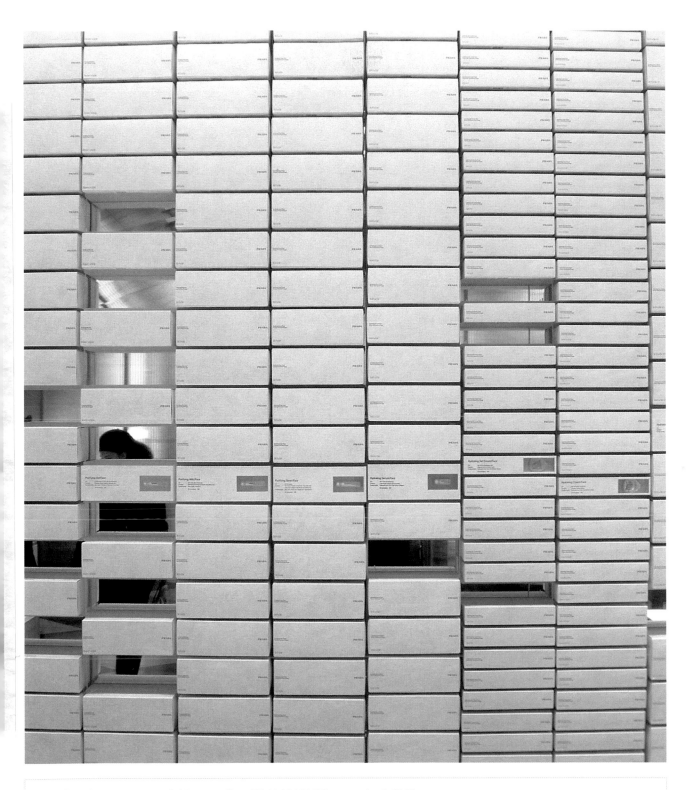

Prada Epicenter New York | Rem Koolhaas/OMA | 2001 | Photography © OMA

Influences

We know how to seduce our clientele, we have decided on the decorative style that will dominate our window and establishment and all the elements are in position. It is time to consider the influences. The store window reflects many of the activities we enjoy doing in our free time.

Elements found in the theater, concerts or films are revealed in the store windows, which become stages where the action develops. They display a product in such a way that it attracts the customer's attention and lures them inside our establishment. Once inside we find ourselves with the star – the product itself – and the design we have chosen conjures up a land of fantasy, removed from reality, where what matters above all else is to seduce the customer. But how is this done? By using all the elements – light, color, furnishings, materials – that are within our reach.

Stores are like a large stage or a film where the action is "invented" around a product causing repercussions and hopefully acceptance in a highly competitive world. As Bertolt Brecht, the German playwright once said: "The theater no longer captivates the audience by creating illusions, making them forget the world and reconciling them with their destiny. Now the theater presents the world so that it can be transformed". The stage work that is carried out in establishments can be likened to that of a theater, and as Brecht says, it creates a world, in many cases a fantasy, that helps customers opt for a particular product. Thanks to this stage work, customers become part of their surroundings, both the store's window and its interior, and begin to see how much they need the product they are being offered.

But stage work and cinema art are not the only influences over the design of store windows and interiors. As we have said in previous chapters, the point of sales has become increasingly important, and every element is considered when trying to attract clientele. Establishments and shopping malls are not just limited to shops as we know them. They can be influenced by their sur-

Issey Miyake London | Stanton Williams | 1999 | Photography © Peter Cook/View

Caramelo Boutique Barcelona | GCA Arquitectes Associats | 2002 | Photography © Jordi Miralles

Mango Barcelona | Damián Sánchez | 2002 | Photography © Joan Mundó

Mango Mataró | Damián Sánchez | 2000 | Photography © Taku

roundings. And so today all sorts of places have a point of sales. In museums, which are witnessing increasing visitor numbers, it is very common to find a gift store where the dominant decor, logically, draws on the museum and its dominant elements. The same occurs in airports, where we find small stores that help passengers to pass the time, and since these establishments usually receive quick visits, the design and decoration must appear casual and the products must be placed where they can be immediately accessed.

Both the shops we find in museums and those found in airports use the same formula as establishments that we all know. If we choose museum-style décor, we display our product throughout the store like, for example, an establishment dedicated to selling footwear, especially sports footwear, or one dedicated to the sale of cell phones. These products are arranged on large panels installed along the walls, in such a way that we feel as if we are at an exhibition. The structure of an airport shop can be seen in a candy store or a tobacconist; places where we do not spend much time and which often have reduced dimensions.

We must not forget that the sales space is becoming more and more important. The customers are now much better prepared and need a place where everything is to their tastes. We want homely places, that have a natural air and are not excessively sophisticated. We must not forget that, thanks to the Industrial Revolution and the development of new technologies, the concept of buying has changed. We no longer merely buy from necessity. Shopping has become a pastime, a recreational activity, and so we need establishments that allow us to relax and enjoy what we are being offered.

Mandarina Duck Barcelona | Fubert S.L. | 2001 | Photography © Eugeni Pons
Factor Dental Barcelona | Manuel Ortiz | 1999 | Photography © Jordi Miralles

Desso Showroom Waalwij | Van Esveld Dierdorp Design Associates | 2001 | Photography © Frank Tielemans

Mango Barcelona | Damián Sánchez | 2000 | Photography © Joan Mundó

Maison Hermès Tokyo | Renzo Piano/Rena Dumas Architecture Intérieure | 2001 | Photography © Michel Denancé

Y's Yohji Yamamoto Boutique Copenhague | Svendborg+Balsborg | 2001 | Photography © Station I/Adam Mørk

Instruments of Seduction

A Captivating Audience

So, we have seen how important it is to seduce customers in order to attract them towards our product, how we can choose a particular decorative style and how establishments can be influenced by different elements and arts. From now on we are going to focus on everything that favors seduction.

Seduction is an art, and it does not depend on what we have but what we do. This means that, in terms of seduction, the product ceases to be the most important factor. Our priority is how we are going to sell the product, the way in which we are going to attract the people and how we are going to decorate and arrange the store window. The latter is the most important in the art of seduction, as customers must be lured using the visual impact that takes place in the first few seconds. Seduction is a psychological art and attempts to make customers believe that this is the product they have spent their time looking for and desiring.

But... how can we seduce? By using the wide variety of materials that are at our disposal when decorating the window. We have already said in previous chapters that the store window must be versatile and must be adaptable to the latest fashions to avoid losing customers. It must be possible to add all elements.

Fortunately, design today has become so important that it allows us to combine different materials and elements in a single window. This gives us a lot of leeway, allowing us to broaden our decorative horizons and make the most of the position and surroundings of the establishment.

There are no rules. Today everything goes, and that is our guarantee that no two window displays are going to be the same. The combination of materials offers a wide range of possibilities and we can, therefore, always come up with something original.

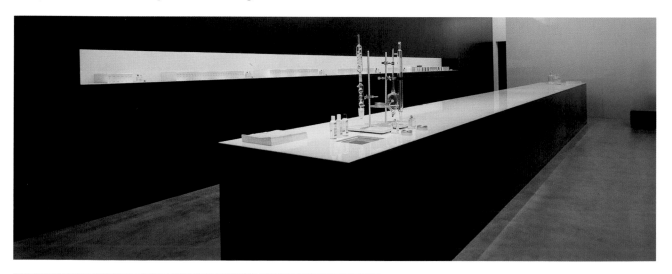

Helmut Lang Parfumerie New York | Gluckman Mayner Architects | 2001 | Photography © Lidia Gould
Jil Sander Paris | Gabellini Associates | 1995 | Photography © Paul Warchol

Camisería Pons Barcelona | Enric Sagnier | 2001 | Photography © Nuria Fuentes

Nicole Farhi Flagship | Gabellini Associates | 1999 | Photography © Paul Warchol

Helmut Lang Boutique New York | Gluckman Mayner Architects | 1997 | Photography © Paul Warchol
Cafe Donna The Martin's Valaoritou Athens | Zege | 2000 | Photography © V. Makris

Desso Showroom Waalwij | Van Esveld Dierdorp Design Associates | 2001 | Photography © Frank Tielemans

Malo Milan | Claudio Nardi | 2001 | Photography © Matteo Piazza

Jigsaw London | John Pawson | 1996 | Photography © John Edward Linden

Light and Color

Both light and color are fundamental aspects in the decoration of spaces, and in terms of store windows their function is of paramount importance. We must be very aware of the location of our establishment because the natural light may play a vital role in favoring the projection of colors that decorate the interior of the window. For example, if the natural light enters through the sides, a dark ceiling may give the window a gloomy appearance, while if the light enters from the front it is advisable that the floor is light. As we have said, the quantity of natural light that enters our window must be well studied because, based on this, some form of artificial lighting will be used.

Once this research has been carried out we need to focus on the artificial lighting, which can be found in abundance in window display decoration, as it affords us greater flexibility through its different intensities. First of all we need to plan what the general lighting will be, to be able to then concentrate on the feature lighting; that which highlights the product on display.

The key to good lighting is that it provides the atmosphere that we have chosen for our window. To do this we need to use what is known as ambient lighting, achieved by arranging lights in the ceiling of the window or using wall lights. Ambient lighting provides a general level of light, which will be similar both in the window and in the establishment. This will let our customers easily and comfortably adapt to both areas, visually speaking. But the ambient lighting in the store window does not usually give enough light for the window to fulfill its objective: to attract the maximum number of customers possible. To do this we need to complete the feature lighting.

Lighting is an instrument of seduction that does not only illuminate the store window to make it visible to potential customers. Its function is also to give emphasis and make the product we are displaying, and some of its possible advantages, stand out.

The key to lighting a specific area or element is to create enough light for potential customers to easily see

Ultimo San Francisco | Gabellini Associates | 1997 | Photography © Paul Warchol

Ferrari Store Maranello | Massimo Iosa Ghini | 2001 | Photography © Santi Caleca

Ferrari Store Maranello | Massimo Iosa Ghini | 2001 | Photography © Santi Caleca

what we wish to show them, Also the installation of feature lighting will give our window a touch of distinction. Another characteristic of feature lighting is that it can be regulated depending on the need and situation. It can be adjusted in order for us to achieve our prime objective. Which lights are the most appropriate for this lighting? We can use fluorescent lights; which consume less energy, or halogen lights, which produce a clear, intense light, allowing us to show the product clearly and without shadows. Thanks to design today, we can combine lights creating contrasts and lighting combinations that make our store window much more attractive.

When we consider color we must remember that it is a highly powerful instrument of seduction that affords us surprising and unimaginable results, as it provides endless different shades that no material can do. But when we talk about color, we are not just referring to the walls and ceiling, we also mean the curtains, the furnishings, the decorations, and, of course, we are referring to the color of our product, which, after all, is what needs to stand out and attract the customers. The color is the first element to attract; its visual impact takes just a few seconds and produces immediate stimulation.

Color is the simplest way to transform a store window in relation to the time of year, or the latest fashions. Every color has its personality, and thanks to this we can achieve window displays that reflect a cold, warm, intimate, serene or modern environment. Through color we can delineate areas within the same space increasing the possibilities our window has to attract. Remember that there are no rules, so combinations of colors are always accepted, as long as we are coher-

Big Net Vienna | René Chavanne | 2001 | Photography © Hélène Bignet

Big Net Vienna | René Chavanne | 2001 | Photography © Hélène Bignet

Emporio Armani Manhasset | Peter Marino | 1996 | Photography © Peter Aaron/Esto

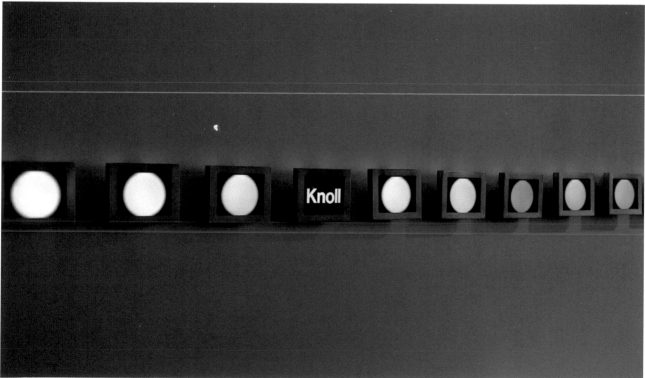

Issey Miyake London | Stanton Williams | 1999 | Photography © Peter Cook/View
Moss New York | Harry Allen & Associates | 1999 | Photography © Mihail Moldoveanu

Castellani Milan | Alfredo Mattesini | Photography © Adriano Vecchio

Amaya Arzuaga Madrid | Francesc Pons | 2000 | Photography © Raimón Solà

ent and favor contrasts. If this is not the case then the window will not accomplish its objective, as if it is excessively garish and there is not structure, instead of attracting customers it will encourage them to look for something that is more visually pleasing.

Color schemes are a way of organizing colors, allowing us to work with them and consider what will be most effective for capturing the public's attention. There are two groups of color schemes; harmonizing and contrasting. Within the harmonizing schemes are monochromatic colors, in other words, those that use different shades and tones of a single color. Using a single color allows us to create a harmonious and serene atmosphere but it can also appear boring, so the life-span of our window display may be much shorter. Within this type of schemes, we also have

analogue colors that are situated in the same area on the color wheel, like for example, purple, red purple and blue purple. These are similar colors and can be easily combined.

When we talk about contrasting color schemes we are referring to the use of colors that are found opposite each other on the color wheel, like for example, green and red. They are colors, which, in theory, are shocking when seen together but dominate window display decoration because they create an exciting effect that immediately catches the attention.

As we mentioned in the introduction to this chapter, there are no rules to follow here. Both the choice of lighting and color is mainly based on our tastes. Light and color are inevitably bound together in order to achieve the desired effect.

Gonzalo Comella Barcelona | GCA Arquitectes Associats | 2000 | Photography © Jordi Miralles

Gonzalo Comella Barcelona | GCA Arquitectes Associats | 2000 | Photography © Jordi Miralles

The Martin's Valaoritou Athens | Zege | 2001 | Photography © V. Makris

The Martin's Valaoritou Athens | Zege | 2001 | Photography © V. Makris

The Martin's Valaoritou Athens | Zege | 2001 | Photography © V. Makris

The Martin's Valaoritou Athens | Zege | 2001 | Photography © V. Makris

The Space

When we talk about store windows we normally mean areas that are quite small. We only have a few meters at our disposal to exhibit our product so we need to make the most of them.

We have already said that stores are often set up on the ground floor of a building, they have no option but to adapt to an environment that has been constantly changing over the years. The installation of an establishment and, more specifically, its exterior decoration is influenced by the style of the building. It must follow the same line because it ought to integrate with its surroundings, that way the customer will see that the store in front of him maintains an architectural structure, which gives a sense of well-being, thereby enticing him to enter.

The window display, logically, also depends on the building that houses it. It is not the same if we have a façade with large windows (ideal for a store window) or if the space has limited possibilities for displaying the product. We may find ourselves with only small openings, the size of a normal window, in which to exhibit our product. In this case the use that we make of the lighting or our choice of color is what will help us to attract customers.

As we have seen, the building that houses our store limits, in some cases to a large degree, the installation of one window display or another. We must follow the structural line and style that is dominant in the building. But when considering the inside of an establishment we have two choices. We could reflect the

Ferragamo New York | Gabellini Associates | 2000 | Photography © Paul Warchol

Camper Showroom Milan | Martí Guixé | 2000 | Photography © Inga Knölke

style of the building in the interior. If it is an old or classical building the decoration may be more romantic, more serious, where light colors prevail, giving a sense of harmony and warmth. On the other hand, if we want to break from this structure or from our surroundings, we could opt for a completely different design that helps to create an unreal atmosphere, one of fantasy, which takes us away from our daily lives. Remember there are no rules. Let your imagination fly and consider the vastdecorative possibilities that are available to you.

Louis Vuitton Beverly Hills | Peter Marino | 1999 | Photography © David Cardelús
Chanel Boutique London | Peter Marino | 2001 | Photography © Paul Warchol

Y's Yohji Yamamoto Boutique Copenhague | Svendborg+Balsborg | 2001 | Photography © Station I/Adam Mørk

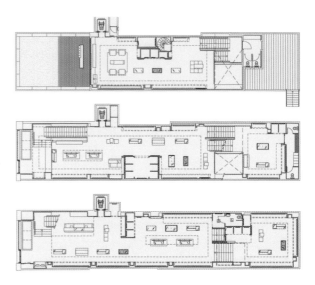

Caramelo Boutique Barcelona | GCA Arquitectes Associats | 2002 | Photography © Jordi Miralles

Caramelo Boutique Barcelona | GCA Arquitectes Associats | 2002 | Photography © Jordi Miralles

Prada Epicenter New York | Rem Koolhaas/OMA | 2001 | Photography © OMA

Materials

Materials are instruments of seduction that almost go unnoticed by the customers, but which play the most important role. Today combining materials is common practice as it increases the store window's possibilities. We must make the customers feel attracted by what we are showing them, so they want to touch and pick up what they are seeing, that's why they will enter our shop and not the one across the street.

The use of a particular material enhances the decorative style that we have chosen for our window display. There is not one which is better than another, and the choice depends on personal tastes, influenced by what we think is most likely to attract attention and by our budget. The dominant material in window displays is glass. This is what relates what is happening in the street with what is happening inside the store, connecting fantasy with reality. On the whole we do not give glass due merit, as we take for granted that it has to there. It can be totally transparent, producing a deep, clean sensation, or this transparency can be combined with opaque areas, which will allow us to create a more mysterious atmosphere, which may be captivating for customers.

However, although, as we have said, glass is the most important element since it is the first thing we see in the display, it is not the only material we find. We need to seduce with other materials, such as metal, that never goes out of fashion and is used on particular situations, (for example, in stores related to bathrooms and kitchens); wood, which has been used for years and increases the sense of warmth and lends a special character to an area that cannot be achieved by other materials; fabrics, which, like with color, allow us to change the appearance of a window display relatively easily; paper, which is being used more and more to cover walls due to its low cost,…

All materials are appropriate for use in store windows, and furthermore, the combination of many of them will lend a unique touch. The choice of one or the other will depend on the context that you have chosen for the product. Again everything we do and every decision we make has to be related to the product.

Prada Epicenter New York | Rem Koolhaas/OMA | 2001 | Photography © OMA

Prada Epicenter New York | Rem Koolhaas/OMA | 2001 | Photography © OMA

Ferragamo Venice | Gabellini Associates | 2000 | Photography © Paul Warchol
Gonzalo Comella Barcelona | GCA Arquitectes Associats | 2000 | Photography © Jordi Miralles
Big Net Vienna | René Chavanne | 2001 | Photography © Hélène Bignet

Camper London | Martí Guixé | 1998 | Photography © Inga Knölke

Furnishings

The use of furnishings greatly improves the display of the product both in the window and inside the establishment. When we talk about furnishings, the idea of the whole prevails over individual elements, in other words, when we decide to use furnishings in the decoration we must bear in mind that they are all interrelated, there must be coherence. We cannot combine a classical table with a modern office chair in the store window. Styles ought to be combined, but in the case of furnishings this is not appropriate as it will surprise the customers and may not make them feel attracted by what we are offering them.

The use of furnishings may be in response to a variety of needs. Perhaps we want to use them solely to support our product, in which case, their use becomes secondary, in other words, it is not an element to which we need to apply too much importance. We can also make their presence relate intimately with the product, i.e. make a particular piece of furniture identify perfectly with the brand, making it unimaginable to think of an establishment offering the same product without using this particular item of furniture. But the use of furnishings also helps to show the qualities of the product inside the store. In certain cases it becomes a front row secondary actor that allows the customers to have contact with the product.

But by furnishings, we do not just mean large elements like tables, chairs, sofas… We need to include all details such as a picture, a vase of flowers, candles, a foot lamp and many other things. All of this combined is what we denominate as furnishings and it gives our window display and establishment a personality that is unique, different from all the rest.

Cafe Donna The Martin's Valaoritou Athens | Zege | 2000 | Photography © V. Makris

The Martin's Valaoritou Athens | Zege | 2001 | Photography © V. Makris

Cappellini Modern Age New York | Photography © Mihail Moldoveanu

Chanel | Peter Marino & Associates | Photography © David Cardelús

Promotion

Until now we have seen physical elements and materials that help us to seduce possible customers. But we should also refer to another instrument of seduction that has at least the same importance as all we have seen till now: the promotion that we would like to carry out for our product.

The product is what matters most, we must never forget that, and what we are offering is not unique. There are many brands producing the same product on the market, which makes it all the more important how we promote ours. We must maximize our clientele. But this is not easy and so to help us we have a marketing team who designs an appropriate advertising structure. We need to communicate, and to do that we cannot leave any stone unturned. However insignificant it may appear it will be relevant when we are trying to sell our product.

It is time to advertise, to put the brand into action. The aim is to convince and seduce the customers and to do this there are numerous strategies to make the customer believe that what he sees is vital, essential for improving his life. This is why it is very common for advertising not to adhere to reality, as its main aim is to manipulate the individual and use all strategies possible to achieve this. It is known as subliminal advertising (that which is shown on a television series, for example) and deceptive advertising (that which does not show all a product's qualities and omits certain characteristics).

Advertising campaigns are vital for attracting customers and even more so today when new technologies are constantly growing and developing. There is no longer just the television, the radio, the newspapers, advertising on paper, or billboards to make the

Desso Showroom Waalwij | Van Esveld Dierdorp Design Associates | 2001 | Photography © Frank Tielemans

Desso Showroom Waalwij | Van Esveld Dierdorp Design Associates | 2001 | Photography © Frank Tielemans

Tardini Store New York | Fabio Novembre | 2001 | Photography © Alberto Ferrero

existence of our product known. The birth and development of the Internet has increased the powers of advertising manifold and has allowed it to reach all sectors of the public. Before the birth of the computer age, advertising could not reach everyone on an equal basis.

As well as all of this we must not forget that advertising uses social models. Not all products are designed for all sectors of the public. The marketing team will be perfectly aware of this and follow a particularly strategy depending on the targeted sector of the public. Advertising understands this fact so clearly that they classify their advertising strategies according to the main social groups, which are then reflected in the advertisements:

Housewives are the aim of most advertising since it is assumed that they watch most television or listen to the most radio, and they are in charge of doing the shopping.

Children because they are potential customers. They play an important role in Christmas advertising campaigns because they are the main targets of the adverts. And their presence is increasingly frequent both in advertisements for toys and products aimed at parents (furniture that boasts security features for children …).

Sports people are targeted by all advertising related to sport and health. They are the potential customers for this type of product (sports clothing, equipment, vitamins …).

The intellectual is the last of our social groups. Their age differs but is always related to men who are financially comfortable, and are often targets of adverts for cars, books, watches …

Advertising leaves no stone unturned. Everything is important to accomplish the aim of seducing customers, to attract their attention and give our product a strong footing in such a highly competitive market.

Cacao Sampaka Barcelona | Antoni Arola | 2001 | Photography © Eugeni Pons
Nicole Farhi Flagship | Gabellini Associates | 1999 | Photography © Paul Warchol

Yves Saint Laurent New York | Gluckman Mayner Architects | 2001 | Photography © Lidia Gould

Shop Window Design: The Latest Trends

Louis Vuitton Paris | Peter Marino | 2005 | Photography © David Cardelús

La Ciénega Tokyo | Hideo Yasui | 1998 | Photography © Nacása & Partners

Fendi Roma | Lazzarini & Pickering | Photography © Matteo Piazza

Tehen New York | Daniel Goldner Architects | Photography © Michael Moran

Giorgio Armani Milan | Claudio Silvestrin Architects | Photography © Matteo Piazza

Malo Milan | Claudio Nardi | 2000 | Photography © Matteo Piazza

Gil Vienna | Propeller Z | 2000 | Photography © Margherita Spiluttini

Jigsaw London | John Pawson | 1996 | Photography © John Edward Linden

René Lezard New York | 1100 Architects | 1997 | Photography © Michael Moran

Amaya Arzuaga | Francesc Pons | 2000 | Photography © Raimón Solà

Antonio Pernas Barcelona | Iago Seara | Photography © Eugeni Pons

Tehen New York | Daniel Goldner Architects | Photography © Michael Moran

Malo Milan | Claudio Nardi | 2000 | Photography © Matteo Piazza

Chanel Paris | Peter Marino | 2003 | Photography © David Cardelús